Zoos

Identifying Propaganda Techniques

Curriculum Consultant: JoAnne Buggey, Ph.D.
College of Education, University of Minnesota

By Terry O'Neill

Greenhaven Press, Inc.
Post Office Box 289009
San Diego, CA 92128-9009

Titles in the opposing viewpoints juniors series:

AIDS   The Palestinian Conflict
Alcohol   Patriotism
Animal Rights   Poverty
Death Penalty   Prisons
Drugs and Sports   Smoking
The Environment   Television
Gun Control   Toxic Wastes
The Homeless   The U.S. Constitution
Immigration   Working Mothers
Nuclear Power   Zoos

Library of Congress Cataloging-in-Publication Data

O'Neill, Terry, 1944–
    Zoos : identifying propaganda techniques / by Terry O'Neill ;
curriculum consultant, JoAnne Buggey.
        p.   cm. — (Opposing viewpoints juniors.)
    Summary: Presents opposing viewpoints about the value of having
zoos and keeping animals in them.
    ISBN 0-89908-600-4
    1. Zoos—Philosophy—Juvenile literature. 2. Zoo animals—
Juvenile literature.   [1. Zoos. 2. Zoo animals.] I. Buggey,
JoAnne. II. Title. III. Series.
QL76.029 1990
590'.74'401—dc20   90-3247
                                                       CIP
                                                        AC

Cover photo: Jerry Howard/Positive Images

CONTENTS

THE PURPOSE OF
THIS BOOK

An Introduction to
Opposing Viewpoints

When people disagree, it is hard to figure out who is right. You may decide one person is right just because the person is your friend or a relative. But this is not a very good reason to agree or disagree with someone. It is better if you try to understand why these people disagree. On what main points do the two people disagree? Read or listen to each person's argument carefully. Separate the facts and opinions that each person presents. Finally, decide which argument best matches what you think. This process, examining an argument without emotion, is part of what critical thinking is all about.

This is not easy. Many things make it hard to understand and form opinions. People's values, ages, and experiences all influence the way they think. This is why learning to read and think critically is an invaluable skill.

Opposing Viewpoints Juniors books will help you learn and practice skills to improve your ability to read critically. By reading opposing views on an issue, you will become familiar with methods people use to attempt to convince you that their point of view is right. And you will learn to separate the authors' opinions from the facts they present.

Each Opposing Viewpoints Juniors book focuses on one critical thinking skill that will help you judge the views presented. Some of these skills are telling fact from opinion, recognizing propaganda techniques, and locating and analyzing the main idea. These skills will allow you to examine opposing viewpoints more easily. The viewpoints are placed in a running debate and are always placed with the pro view first.

What Are Propaganda Techniques?

Propaganda is information presented in an attempt to influence people. In this Opposing Viewpoints Juniors book you will be asked to identify and study several common propaganda techniques. Some of these techniques appeal to your ability to think logically while others appeal to your emotions. As an example, a car salesperson who is telling you about a small economy car may say, "This car gets much better gas mileage than any other car in its class." The salesperson's argument is based on his belief that you will make your car-buying decision logically. You will compare practical considerations such as mileage and initial cost. Another example is a car salesperson who is telling you about a snazzy Maserati: "This car is the best-looking, fastest car ever made." Her argument for buying the Maserati is based on her belief that you are considering such a car not for its practical qualities but because it excites you and is a status symbol.

In the examples above, the objective of both salespeople is to encourage you to buy a car. Both try to get you to focus on the most appealing quality of their cars—economy in the first example, flashiness in the second. Both ignore the disadvantages of their cars. In both cases, making a wise buying decision would mean getting more information. Since the car salespeople's objective is to get you to buy *their* car, you would need more objective sources, such as *Consumer Reports* magazine, to find out more facts.

DISTRACTING THE READER

All propaganda techniques, like those used by the car salespeople, distract the listener or reader from the complete picture. People who use propaganda techniques encourage you to look only at the factors that are important to accepting their argument as true.

Authors and speakers often use misleading propaganda techniques instead of offering legitimate proof for their arguments. The propaganda will be offered as a reason to believe the argument, but in reality will be weak, distracting, or irrelevant reasons. This Opposing Viewpoints Juniors book will focus on telling the difference between legitimate reasons to believe a particular argument and propaganda techniques that are used to mislead or distract you.

It is important to learn to recognize these techniques, especially when reading and evaluating differing opinions. This is because people who feel strongly about an issue use many of these techniques when attempting to persuade others to agree with their opinion. Some of these persuasive techniques may be relevant to your decision to agree or not, but others will not be. It is important to sift through the information, weeding the proof from the false reasoning.

While there are many types of propaganda techniques, this book will focus on four of them. These are *testimonial, card stacking, scare tactics* and *slanted words and phrases.* Examples of these techniques are given below:

Testimonial—quoting or paraphrasing an authority or celebrity to support one's own argument. Often, the celebrity is not qualified to express an opinion on the subject. For example, movie stars are often used to recommend a product they may know nothing about. An actor may be dressed in a white medical coat to recommend a pain medication in a television commercial. The producers of the commercial believe you will assume the actor in a white medical coat is a doctor. They hope you will buy the pain medication because you trust doctors' opinions. But the truth is that the actor is not a doctor, has no knowledge of medicine, and is in no position to express an informed opinion. The commercial is deceptive—it asks you to accept the advice of someone who is not a true authority on the topic.

Testimonials can be used in a positive way as well. If the person quoted is truly an authority on the subject being talked about, the testimonial can support an argument. Quoting comedian Richard Pryor about how drugs almost ruined his life is an example of a testimonial that presents a legitimate reason to believe drugs can be dangerous. Pryor *is* an authority on this subject and can give advice based on his personal experience.

Card stacking—using half-truths or whole truths in order to make one's own argument seem strongest. Card-stacking techniques include distorting or twisting facts, giving only the facts that are favorable to your argument, or quoting someone incompletely or out of context.

An example is "four out of five dentists surveyed recommend sugarless gum for their patients who chew gum." At first, this statement seems to say that most dentists believe people should chew sugarless gum. In fact, this statement is an example of card stacking for a number of reasons: For one thing, we do not know how many dentists were surveyed. If only five were surveyed, this statistic is not very meaningful. Also, this statement is actually saying that dentists recommend sugarless gum only if their patients already chew gum. That is not the same as saying everyone should chew sugarless gum.

Scare tactics—the threat that if you do not do or believe this, something terrible will happen. People using this technique write or say alarming words and phrases to persuade you to believe their argument.

An example is "illegal immigration endangers every worker in the United States." The person quoted does not say *how* illegal immigration will endanger everyone. The purpose of the statement is to scare you into believing his argument. The person wants you to make a decision based on fear about the issue, not on logical reasoning.

Slanted words and phrases—words that have opinions or emotions built into them instead of words that are more neutral. For example, *slum* or *tenement* conveys the idea of a place that is dirty, crumbling, and very poor. But *low-income high-rise* suggests something newer, cleaner, and a bit fancier. A politician who has been responsible for getting more low-income housing built would use the last term when describing these buildings. A political activist who believes the housing is not an improvement may use the words "slum" and "tenement" to describe them.

For another example, think of a time when you noticed that your watch was not where you usually leave it. You might simply describe the situation: "My watch is not on my dresser." Or you might use slanted language: "My watch was *stolen* from my dresser."

SOUND REASONING VS. PROPAGANDA

When reading differing arguments, then, there is a lot to think about. Are the authors giving sound reasons for their points of view? Or do they distort the importance of their arguments through card stacking, use testimonials deceptively, or play on your fear and emotions through scare tactics?

We asked two students to give their opinions on the zoo issue. Look for examples of testimonial, card stacking, scare tactics, and slanted words and phrases in their arguments:

I like zoos.

One of my favorite places is the zoo. It's so neat to see animals that you can't see anyplace else. My grandma says today's zoos are great. She says that when she was my age, zoo animals lived in small cement cages with bars. The animals had only a little space to move around. They only had hard, cold concrete to lie on. But zoos today are really different. It's almost like being where the animals live in the wild. Our zoo has a cat habitat where lions and tigers can prowl through the jungle. It has a big seal pool that looks almost like a little ocean. It has rocks for the seals to sunbathe on and lots of clean water for them to swim in. I think animals today probably like being in the zoo. It's like being at home, only easier. In the zoo they are fed, and they don't have to worry about other animals attacking them. Which is better—having zoos where we can go and see them and learn about animals, or not having zoos and having animals become extinct? I think zoos are our best choice.

I hate zoos.

Zoos are terrible places. Animals are kidnapped from their homes and are brought to zoos just so people can stare at them. I know that zoos look nicer than they used to. Many zoos are designed to look like the places the animals really came from. But they are only imitations. No zoo can give the elephants and jaguars miles and miles of jungle to roam in, like they would have in their real homes. Zoos make animals lose their natural instincts, too. Zoo animals don't have to catch their own food, so they forget how to do it. This means that the animals we see in zoos are sort of imitations. The zoo monkey is not anything like a real monkey. The zoo monkey learns to do the things that the zookeepers like and that the people come to see. You could say that zoos are killing the real animals. Plus, some animals in even the nicest zoos get sick and die just because they are away from their natural home. If we keep building zoos, we will keep killing the animals. I think all zoos should be banned.

Carl and Deirdre have very different opinions about zoos. Both use examples of propaganda techniques in their arguments:

Carl:

TESTIMONIAL

My grandmother says today's zoos are great.

CARD STACKING

Which is better—having zoos where we can go and see them and learn about them or not having zoos and having a lot of animals become extinct? [*The reader is given only two choices, one of them obviously bad and the other better. The reader is almost forced to agree with Carl and choose the first option.*]

Deirdre:

SLANTED WORDS OR PHRASES

Animals are *kidnapped* . . .
[Today's zoos] are *only imitations.*

SCARE TACTICS

If we keep building zoos, we will keep killing animals.

Both Carl and Deirdre think they are right about zoos. What do you think? What do you conclude about zoos from these two sample viewpoints? Why?

As you continue to read through the viewpoints in this book, try keeping a tally like the one above to compare the authors' arguments.

CHAPTER 1

PREFACE: Do Zoos Provide Wholesome Entertainment?

Each year 125 million people visit American zoos. These people come for many reasons. But most agree that the main reason is entertainment.

At the zoo, people can see animals up close they will never see anyplace else. People like to see the giraffe reach to the top of a tree and grab a leafy twig to eat. They love the koalas that peer shyly around the tree they are hugging. They laugh at the monkeys' antics, whether playing on a jungle gym or swinging through real trees. They thrill at the lion's roar and applaud the performing seal.

But should people be enjoying these things? Some people believe that zoo animals are little more than slaves. They think that the people who come to see the animals are cruel. They think that people should realize that monkeys, lions, giraffes, and other animals are not happy being displayed in a zoo. Animals should be left in their native homes and people should learn about them in other ways.

Whether or not zoos are good places is a deeply emotional issue. The people on both sides use propaganda techniques to promote their views. As you read the following viewpoints, watch for examples of scare tactics, card stacking, slanted words or phrases, and testimonial.

Editor's Note: This viewpoint argues that zoos are harmless and enjoyable. As you read, examine the type of information the viewpoint gives to attempt to persuade you that zoos are fun. Does the author used slanted words and phrases to sway your emotions?

Walking down the wooden path, the Franklin family peers eagerly through the woods that surround them. They are exploring Wolf Woods, a new exhibit at their city zoo. They hope to catch a glimpse of the wolf family that has recently had cubs. At first they see nothing but woods and an occasional squirrel. They hear birds chirping and the scurrying of other small creatures. Suddenly the youngest daughter stops. Her eyes wide, she tugs her mother's sleeve. "Look," she whispers. "I see one."

The family halts, straining their eyes against the darkness of the thick trees. There. Each of them sees the timberwolf, standing perfectly still a little way up the hill, looking majestic, its golden eyes seeming to pierce their own. The wolf watches them. With breaths held, they watch it. Seeming to sense that there is no danger, the wolf finally turns away and quietly melts into the woods.

Here the author is not simply describing the wolf in an objective way. *Majestic* is a slanted word.

The Franklins burst into chatter. This was not what they had come to see, but it was exciting nevertheless. This is the first wolf any of them have ever seen outside of movies and they find it hard to believe how excited it has made them. Mr. Franklin reminds his family of what they had read about the wolves at the beginning of the exhibit—information about the wolves' pack habits, how they behave when they see potential enemies, what they eat, how they raise their young.

The Franklins never did see the wolf babies, but a little later they saw other animal families—parents and their young—in other exhibits in their local zoo.

This is one of the things today's zoos are able to do well. They allow people the privilege of viewing animals in environments very much like the animals' native ones, but under safe conditions. Today's zoo designers strive for the reality that thrills. Jon Coe is a Philadelphia professor and zoo designer. He says, "I judge the effectiveness of a zoo exhibit in the pulse rate of the zoo goer. We can design a zoo that will make the hair stand up on the back of your neck."

Here the author uses the opinion of an authority—a zoo designer—to reinforce the idea that zoos are entertaining. Which propaganda technique is this?

Not many families can afford to travel to Africa in the hope of catching a glimpse of lions prowling the tall grasses or lazing in the sun. Not many can travel to Brazil in hope of glimpsing colorful parrots and the elusive jaguars in the rainforest. Not many even get to see a real prairie dog town in the southwestern United States. But everybody can travel to the zoo.

This paragraph is an example of card stacking. The author emphasizes a number of things that "most families cannot do." She makes zoos seem like the only alternative to these things.

At the zoo, people not only learn facts about the animals they see. They can also spend many hours with one of the most enjoyable and wholesome forms of entertainment.

What could be more amusing than watching the little capuchin monkeys racing madly among the trees, shrieking and chattering? What could be more touching than seeing the Japanese snow monkeys cuddling their young just as humans do their own infants? What could be more colorful than seeing the peacocks preening and the flamingos showing off their radiant colors? What could be more delightful than watching the sea lions and porpoises perform, defying gravity as they leap out of the water?

In this paragraph the author uses a lot of words that make the animals seem almost human: The snow monkeys *cuddle* their young, the flamingos *show off*. These slanted words make the reader identify with the animals.

Since the vast majority of people lives in cities, many have never seen living animals except dogs, cats, and pigeons. At the zoo, this can be remedied. Many zoos have a "petting zoo," designed to allow children to mingle with harmless animals. The children can pet a young llama, give food pellets to a rabbit, and dodge the gently butting head of a small goat. Most zoos also have "zoo talks" where a keeper or volunteer brings exotic animals into reach. Sometimes zoo visitors are allowed to pet a leopard cub or feel a snake's scales and rippling muscles.

In some zoos, the keepers keep their elephants and camels well-exercised by allowing visitors to ride them. The child who is boosted onto the back of an elephant feels thrilled and deliciously scared. No video game can compare with this.

The zoo is a place people can go to see and feel a part of the best parts of our world. *Time* magazine writer David Bjerklie says, "Zoos provide a decent, delightful place for animals and people to meet and, with luck, fall in love." Every family should go to the zoo.

What slanted words does David Bjerklie use in his testimonial?

Are zoos entertaining?

List three ways the author says zoos are entertaining. Do you agree with the author that they are *wholesome* entertainment?

Editor's Note: This viewpoint argues that zoos are harmful to animals and are not enjoyable places. As you read, be aware of how the author attempts to persuade you. Take note of which propaganda techniques are used.

When the author says the animals have been *stolen from their homes,* what propaganda technique is she using?

What slanted word or phrase does the author use in the last sentence of this paragraph?

By quoting Michael W. Fox, what propaganda technique is the author using?

When you visit a zoo, what do you see? Do you see happy animals living normal animal lives? No. You see animals that have been stolen from their homes and put on display. No animal should live like this.

Some people think that zoos are educational. Yes, the zoo is a place to see animals that you might never see anyplace else. But this is not a truly good reason for having zoos. The animals in zoos are not like the animals in a natural environment. So whatever educational values zoos might seem to have is lost. Zoo visitors are not seeing the animals in a realistic light.

Most people think zoos are good, clean entertainment. But put yourself in the place of the animals. How would you feel about being on display nearly every moment of your life? How would you feel about being unable to do the things you love most? How would you feel about being at the mercy of a zookeeper?

Let's take the lions as an example of "entertainment" at a zoo. They are majestic beasts, beautiful to behold. What is their life like at a zoo? How many times have you seen a lion pacing and pacing in a small cage? Even the better zoos are not that great. There the lions wear a dirt path all around the fenced-in area. Is this entertainment?

Michael W. Fox, head of the United States Humane Society, recalls a beautiful panther he saw in a zoo when he was a child. The panther "was in constant motion. Her liquid form brushed across the front of the cage." Then it brushed around some artificial rocks and a tree stump toward the back of the enclosure. The panther rebounded off a ceramic-tiled wall to again brush the front of the cage. "The pattern of movement within the confines of the cage [was] so repetitive....that she was more like a perpetual motion machine than a sentient [conscious] being."

In remembered horror he adds, "Then I saw the blood: a streak of blood down her left thigh, draining from an open sore that would never heal until the cat was freed from the hypnotic lines she traced. Each scraping turn around the tree trunk kept the sore open like a broken heart bleeding for the loss of all that was wild and free.... Perhaps she was engaged in a ritual form of suicide, gradually grinding and rubbing and shredding her body to pieces in order to free the wild spirit within."

Mr. Fox is convinced that zoos are far from entertaining. He thinks they are dangerous to the animals.

Is it entertainment to enjoy the beauty of an exotic bird that cannot fly because its wings have been clipped or bound to prevent escape? Is it entertainment to watch, half-horrified, half-amused, the monkeys and gorillas who play with their own waste because they are bored and frustrated? Is it entertainment to watch a lone wolf, who is used to living in a pack, huddled in the back of a cage? Is it entertainment to ooh and ahh over a litter of baby rabbits when we know full well that most of them will be killed or sold to research labs or to roadside "zoos" because the zoo does not have room for a dozen more adults?

No, the zoo is not an appropriate place for entertainment. Animals deserve the same freedom that humans do. If we want to see exotic animals for ourselves, it is best to see them in the beautifully photographed films of the National Geographic Society and other similar organizations. They do their best to film the animals in a non-disturbing and ethical way. If you care about animals, stay home from the zoo.

Does Mr. Fox use any slanted words? Which ones?

What propaganda techniques does the author use in this paragraph?

"It's Bob, all right...but look at those vacuous eyes, that stupid grin on his face —he's been domesticated, I tell you."

Do zoos treat animals unfairly?

The author of this viewpoint uses three main propaganda techniques—testimonial, card stacking, and slanted words. Do you think she proves that zoos are not entertaining? Which of her arguments did you find most convincing?

Identifying Propaganda Techniques

Read the two viewpoints on zoos as entertainment. Then make a chart similar to the one made for Carl and Deirdre on page 10. List four examples of propaganda techniques from each viewpoint. (It is possible that you will not find all four techniques in each viewpoint.) You may use a technique more than once. A chart is started for you below:

Viewpoint 1:

TESTIMONIAL

Jon Coe says zoo designers can make people's hair stand on end.

SCARE TACTICS

CARD STACKING

SLANTED WORDS OR PHRASES

Viewpoint 2:

TESTIMONIAL

SCARE TACTICS

CARD STACKING

SLANTED WORDS OR PHRASES

Zoo animals were *stolen from their homes.*

After completing your chart, answer the following questions: Which article used the most propaganda techniques? Which argument did you find the most convincing? Why?

CHAPTER

PREFACE: Do Zoos Treat Animals Humanely?

People concerned with animal rights are very vocal. Some think that zoos should be abolished. Others say that today's zoos are, for the most part, humane homes for animals. These groups disagree over two main ideas. One is over care of the animals. The other is over the philosophy of whether animals should be put into foreign and artificial environments.

Those who argue that zoos maltreat animals point to a number of examples. These include zoos that keep animals in small concrete cages, often with heavy metal bars. They point to animals that have nothing to do all day but sit in their cages and wait to be fed. They point to zoos that do not clean the cages adequately or often enough. They point to zoos that separate baby animals from their parents. And they point to instances of physical cruelty such as beating lions or elephants "to keep them in line." Zoo critics also say that many zoos overbreed certain animals. Then they are left with a surplus that they cannot house. The zoos get rid of the animals any way they can. Sometimes they sell them to other zoos. Sometimes they sell them to dealers who then sell tham to the entertainment industry or to research labs. Sometimes the zoos simply kill the animals.

Those who favor zoos say that these kinds of cruelty are rare in today's zoos. Zoos must meet certain guidelines that are established by regulations, both from the government and from their own organizations. People who favor zoos also argue that animals are not people. An animal that is kept well-fed and healthy does not feel the loss of freedom that some people fear it does. An animal can be just as content living in captivity as living in the wild. Perhaps the animal can be even happier in a zoo because it no longer faces the difficulties of survival in the wild. Zoo supporters point out that animals have a much higher survival rate in zoos than they do in their native habitats.

The next two viewpoints debate whether zoos treat animals humanely. Notice the propaganda techniques used in each viewpoint. Consider whether the propaganda techniques add to or detract from the arguments.

VIEWPOINT 3   Zoos treat animals humanely

Editor's Note: This viewpoint argues that zookeepers want to make sure animals are treated humanely and make every attempt to ensure they lead comfortable and healthy lives. The author believes zoos have changed greatly to improve living conditions as well as knowledge about animals. What types of propaganda techniques does the author use to support this case?

Does Mr. Amory sound like an appropriate person to provide a testimonial on this topic? Does his statement prove the author's point? Why or why not?

Are there any slanted words in this paragraph?

What propaganda technique is being used in this paragraph?

Many people are critical of zoos. But today's zoos are not the ugly concrete cages of the past. Even Cleveland Amory, who started a worldwide organization called The Fund for Animals, believes zoos can be humane. He says, "Once upon a time there was no such thing as a best zoo.... [But] times have changed.... Bars have given way to moats.... You see animals who, if not born free, at least run free. And you see them in their native habitats, or at least reasonable facsimiles [imitations]."

These new zoos are designed in a style called *landscape immersion*. This means that the environments in the exhibits contain not only major animals. They also have carefully designed landscapes that include many native trees, shrubs, and smaller animals. The exhibits are designed so realistically that visitors feel as though they are actually in Africa, the Brazilian jungles, the southwest deserts, and so forth. Visitors cannot see any bars, cages, or other artificial things. In fact, visitors often feel as if the tigers are stalking them, a snake could drop out of the next tree, or they could run into a gorilla on the path.

In the Washington Park Zoo in Portland, Oregon, underwater machines create imitation ocean currents. These currents let penquins from Peru find food exactly like they do in their homeland. In the Minnesota Zoo, the beavers cut down trees to acquire a winter food supply and make their dams. An article in *Newsweek* magazine reports that in Tropic World at the Brookfield Zoo outside Chicago, eleven daily rainstorms "prompt the monkeys to drop from their vines and scamper for cover amid cliffs." These zoos are not designed only for the benefit of the visitors. They are built for the animals.

Despite the new naturalism in zoo design, some critics claim that zoos are still prisons for animals. But long-time zookeeper and animal lover Gerald Durrell says, "Animals [in the wild] have strict territories that are governed by three things: food, water, and sex. Provide all these [a zoo] and the animals will stay there," secure and happy.

What propaganda technique is being used in this paragraph? Is it effective in supporting the author's point of view?

Zoos want to keep animals happy for several reasons. One is that most zoos today see part of their mission as educational. They want their visitors to see what the animals and what their native environments are really like. A listless monkey crouched in the corner of his cage and a bored lion mindlessly pacing do not give a good idea of what the animals are really like.

A second reason is that most zoos want to help preserve endangered species, and only happy, healthy animals will mate. A third, practical, reason is that natural exhibits are exotic and exciting, and this makes visitors happy, thus increasing the zoo's income.

The author lists several reasons zoos *want* to keep the animals happy. Do these reasons convince you that zoos are humane places?

A fourth reason is that most zoo people—directors, keepers, and scientists—love animals. This is the reason they have chosen their professions. They do everything they can to keep their animals content.

It is rare today, at least in the better zoos, to see sick and listless animals. Zookeepers know how to prevent animals from catching diseases. They know how to prepare exactly the kinds of food animals like and need. For example, at the Lincoln Park Zoo in Chicago, zoo cooks prepare food like "Tarantula's Treat" for the tarantulas. It contains crickets as well as calcium to help the tarantulas stay healthy. Also, zookeepers have improved exhibit areas that let the animals act as they would in the wild.

Today's zoos make visitors happy. But most important, they make animals happy.

Do zoos treat animals in a humane way?

List three "proofs" the author uses to show that zoos treat animals properly. Do these proofs seem to you to be objective or stacked in favor of the author's opinion? Do you feel the author is ignoring the other side of the argument? Explain. Do you find the arguments in this viewpoint convincing? Why or why not?

ZOOS **19**

Editor's Note: There have been a few well-publicized cases in the media on how poorly zoos treat animals. These articles have caused people to question whether zoos give animals the right food, decent places to live, and enough stimulation. In this viewpoint, the author quotes many experts to prove the point that zoos treat animals inhumanely. Is it a persuasive case?

No matter how nice a zoo looks to the ordinary visitor, it is not a place that is good for animals.

Some zoos are outright cruel. The elephant is one kind of animal that is often treated badly because, to some people, its size makes it seem dangerous. Many zookeepers believe that the only way to control an elephant is to beat it or to poke it with the sharp hooked stick, called an *ankus,* that elephant keepers carry.

Is this an example of a testimonial? Explain.

Saul Kitchener is director of the San Francisco Zoological Gardens. He has said, "How do you get a 10,000-pound elephant's attention? Hit him, that's how." If that is the only way to control an animal, the zoo should not keep an elephant. Hitting an innocent animal should be forbidden.

Reread the first three paragraphs. Are they objective or card stacking? Explain.

Another way zoos are cruel is by breeding too many baby animals. Zoos like to have a lot of them because the zoo visitors think baby animals are cute. More people will come to the zoo, and the zoo will make more money. But what happens when all these babies grow up? There is not enough room in the zoo to keep all of these adult animals. So they must get rid of them.

This paragraph emphasizes zoo babies. *Why is this an example of card stacking?*

Some zoos simply kill the extra tigers, monkeys, bears, and anteaters. Some sell them to roadside zoos and other places that do not take good care of the animals. Some sell them to research laboratories that are known for treating animals badly. Some kill them and give them to other animals as food.

A critic of the Detroit zoo agrees. Ann Klosowski, president of the Michigan Coalition for Animals, says that the zoo "regularly allows lions to breed, and then [they] euthanize [put to death] the cubs as soon as they mature and begin to show signs of aggression toward their mother."

Is euthanize *a slanted word?*

Some zoos are cruel in more subtle ways. They do not beat or kill their animals. But they make them live in unnatural surroundings that cause the animals to become depressed and sick. If zoo animals are healthy and content, they should not be sleeping *every* time you visit them. All animals nap at times during the day, but healthy animals should also be seen playing, exercising, and interacting with other animals.

Fortunately the old, really terrible zoos are dying away. They were nothing more than tiny cement cages with bars. Both large and small animals were confined to these cruel cages for their entire lives.

Nowadays, most zoos attempt to make the surroundings look something like the animals' original homes. Some zoos use things like playground jungle gyms for the monkeys to play on. Some use cement trees and rocks and small swimming pools for the bears and alligators. Some even create very large enclosures that give visitors the feeling that they are actually in the jungle.

But the animals know the difference. A tiger has miles of its own territory to prowl in Africa. It stalks prey and kills its own food. In even the nicest zoos, it cannot do either of these things. At most, it might have an acre or so to roam, always within sight of the visitors. The tiger is fed dead meat. It does not get the pleasure or the exercise of catching its own food. In some zoos, the great cat is able to watch its natural prey all day. The zebras and gazelles are in sight. But hidden moats and fences keep the tiger from reaching them. The zoo is teasing and frustrating it.

What do you think happens to animals forced to live under these conditions? Many of them sicken and die. Many of them refuse to mate or do other activities they would do in the wild.

No matter how kind the zoo people intend to be, they have robbed these innocent creatures of their natural living space. Zoos are cruel places.

© Zoological Society of San Diego

What propaganda technique is used in this paragraph?

Here the author tells about the terrible things that can happen to animals in zoos. She is using scare tactics.

Are zoos cruel to animals?

List three arguments the author uses to prove that zoos are cruel. Are these convincing to you?

After reading viewpoints 3 and 4, which one do you think presents its arguments most effectively? Which do you agree with more? Give two reasons to explain why.

Identifying Propaganda Techniques

This activity will allow you to practice identifying the propaganda techniques you have been learning in this book. The statements below focus on the subject matter of this chapter—how humanely zoos treat animals. Read each statement and consider it carefully. *Mark an S for any statement you believe is an example of scare tactics, a C for any statement that is card stacking, a T for any statement that is a testimonial, and a W for any statement that relies on slanted words or phrases.*

If you are doing this activity as a member of a class or group, compare your answers with other class or group members. You may find that others have different answers than you do. Listening to the reasons others give for their answers can help you in identifying propaganda techniques.

EXAMPLE: Animals that are forced to live in zoos become depressed, and sick, and then die.

ANSWER: *S*—scare tactic (The writer is trying to make us think that zoos, by their very nature, cause animals to die.)

Answer

1. Cleveland Amory wants to protect animals, and he agrees that zoos can be good places.   _____

2. Today's zoos are wonderful places filled with happy, healthy animals.   _____

3. Petting zoos are filled with dozens of cute, cuddly baby animals that will soon be put to death.   _____

4. Places like the Brookfield Zoo make animals truly feel at home. Neither the animals nor the zoo visitors can tell any difference between the real rainforest and the zoo's rainforest, for example.   _____

5. Mr. Michael Fox believes that zoos treat animals in cruel ways.   _____

6. Zoos are not fair to animals when they keep them locked up in small, unnatural environments where they can do nothing but pace hopelessly.   _____

3

PREFACE: Can Zoos Protect Endangered Species?

David Bjerklie wrote an article about zoos for *Time* magazine. He reported that between the first and seventeenth centuries A.D., several animals species became extinct each year. But that number is growing to almost unbelievable proportions. Bjerklie says that during the 1990s, "the extinction rate may reach several species an hour," every hour around the clock. These disappearing species include ones most of us do not even know about, much less worry about—certain kinds of insects, bacteria, and fish. But they also include more familiar animals such as snow leopards, California condors, and monk seals. Regardless of the species, the numbers are frightening. What can be done to save these animals?

To some people, zoos are the answer. With today's technology, animals' native habitats can be duplicated in almost every detail. The zoo specialists can watch over endangered animals, protecting them from natural enemies, such as predators and disease, and also from hunting, pollution, and deforestation. In addition, today's zoos are able to perform breeding miracles. They can help animals breed and increase in captivity even when they have been unable to survive in the wild.

But there are those who object to using the zoo to save endangered species. Some say that extinction is a normal part of nature. Zoos should not interfere with this process. Others say zoos cannot take on this job for practical reasons. Zoos do not have the space or the resources (knowledge, people, money) to succeed at such a huge task.

More and more zoos today are trying to preserve endangered species. Are they right to do so? Examine the arguments in the following two viewpoints and see which side you think is right.

Editor's Note: As the rainforests continue to be threatened and people take over more and more of the land that animals once occupied, many animals are in danger of extinction. In this viewpoint, the author argues that zoos are a good way to combat this extinction. As you read, be aware of the propaganda techniques the author presents.

In a few years, zoos may be the only places in the world where you can see certain kinds of animals. Colin Rawlins of the Zoological Society in London says, "Ultimately zoos may provide the last refuge for many species of animals which face extinction in the wild."

Norman Myers is a professor and consultant on the environment in England and the Netherlands. He claims that in the past 600 million years, the average rate of extinction has been one species per year. But today between one and several thousand species become extinct each year. If things continue as they are, he says, by the year 2000 there may be as many as one hundred species extinctions every day. This means that up to one-third of all the species living today will become extinct in the next few decades.

Is Norman Myers using scare tactics in this paragraph?

ZOO SUCCESSES WITH ENDANGERED SPECIES

This table shows some of the successes zoos have had in breeding endangered species. The number at the bottom of each bar shows how many animals existed in the wild before zoos got involved. The number at the top of the bar shows how many animals existed in 1988 because of the breeding efforts of zoos.

Some of these animals have been reintroduced to the wild; others have no natural habitat to return to or do not yet have sufficient numbers to assure survival in the wild.

Species	1988 total	Wild before
Wisent (European bison)	2,500	0
NeNe (Hawaiian goose)	2,050	30
Pere David's deer	1,500	0
Golden lion tamarin	600	90
Przewalski's horse	550	0
Arabian oryx	323	0
Black-footed ferret	125	17
Rail	95	10
Kingfisher	46	26

It is no secret that many kinds of animals are disappearing from the earth, mostly because of people. People hunt animals, even when they are rare. People have hunted such creatures as the dodo bird and the carrier pigeon until there is not a single one left in existence. They have hunted other animals, such as the buffalo, until there are only a very few left.

Besides hunting, people do other things that wipe out animal species. People pollute the water animals need to drink. People cut down the forests and plow the fields that animals live in. By doing these things, people destroy the places many animals live. When the animals no longer have homes, they die.

It is probably impossible to stop this destruction. We do the things we do because we need to. There are more of us, so we need more land. Many of the products we need cause pollution. So we must find another way to save the animals.

Do you agree with the ideas in this paragraph—that it is probably impossible to change people's habits?

The best way is zoos. William Conway of the New York Zoological Society says, "No large wild animal will persist long into the future unless cared for" by people. And author Elspeth Huxley says, "We are faced with stark alternatives. Either we breed in captivity the ever-increasing number of animal species threatened with extinction in the wild, or they vanish forever."

What propaganda techniques is Elspeth Huxley using?

Some kinds of animals would be extinct today if it were not for zoos. David M. Kennedy is a writer at Harvard University. He reports that the Arabian oryx was on the brink of extinction because of hunters. "But the international zoo community stepped in," he says. Zoos "set up an intensive breeding program for a few wild oryx from the Arabian peninsula. . . . By the early 1980s more than three hundred of these antelopes were living in zoos, and in 1982 fourteen were released outside the town of Jiddat al Harasis [in Oman]. So far they have flourished and multiplied under the protection of the Sultan." Thanks to the intervention of zoos, the endangered Arabian oryx is back in its natural habitat and increasing. With luck, in a few more years it will no longer be endangered.

Another example is the rail, a kind of bird from the island of Guam. The rail population was down to only ten in the whole world before zoos helped them out. Miraculously, zoos were able to breed rails. In one year, they brought up the world population to ninety-seven. After a few more years, the rail might not be endangered any longer.

What slanted word is used in this paragraph?

As these two examples show, one of the main ways zoos preserve species is by breeding them in captivity where they are protected from threats such as human hunters, loss of natural habitat, and death from natural enemies. Zoos have been able to breed animals extremely well. Here are some of the ways zoos accomplish this:

1. Many zoos are members of the American Association of Zoological Parks and Aquariums (AAZPA). This organization keeps detailed records of the animals in zoos around the country. It keeps records of their blood lines, their success at breeding, and the ways their offspring turn out. In this way, zookeepers who want to breed certain animals can find suitable matches at other zoos. They can work out transfers and loans of animals. Today it is not unusual to see a story in the newspaper about a hippopotamus or a mountain gorilla being sent across the country or even across the world to mate with another zoo's animal.

2. Zoo scientists have made great strides in artificial insemination and in vitro fertilization. In other words, they can put the sperm of a male kangaroo from one zoo into the female in another zoo to make her pregnant. Or, in the case of a female bear who has had difficulty becoming pregnant, they can remove her egg and mix it in a lab container with a male bear's sperm; then they replace the fertilized egg into the female bear.

You have probably read about, or perhaps even known of, animals that "mother" a baby from an entirely different species. For example, sometimes a chicken is tricked into hatching a duck egg and then carries out the responsibilities of mothering the little duckling. Some zoos have gone a step further and have placed a fertilized embryo from one species into the body of another. In England, a zebra embryo was transplanted into a Welsh pony mare. The pony bore the zebra baby and raised it as her own. In Los Angeles, the embryo of a rare bongo antelope was implanted into an eland, another kind of antelope. In this way the bongo population was increased.

These kinds of technological advances are necessary because animals do not always breed according to the schedules humans want to follow. Nate Flesness is the director of the International Species Inventory System (ISIS) that keeps track of animal locations and breeding records. He says, "You may buy a male rhino an air ticket and get him somewhere only to find that the female doesn't like him." Thus technology helps rare or delicate species to be reproduced under the best conditions. This helps ensure the survival of the species.

Another way zoos help preserve endangered species is by rescuing animals whose natural environment is being destroyed. William Conway is the director of the New York Zoological Society. He points out that the tropical rainforest is being lost at the rate of fifty acres every minute. This loss is not going to stop, he says.

The rainforests are home to thousands of species of animals. These include the beautiful big cats—jaguars and cheetahs—as well as rare species of birds and insects that live nowhere else in the world. Zoos are able to create artificial rainforests with plants and climates almost identical to the real forests in South America and elsewhere. Thus it becomes possible to move these rare, delicate creatures to zoo rainforests and keep the species alive. If someday the real rainforests are able to be reforested, the preserved species will be reintroduced there.

Without the efforts of zoos, many important species would die out. Roger Wheater is director of the Zoological Society of Scotland. He asks, "Can we seriously contemplate a world without elephant, rhinoceros, Arabian oryx, or a multitude of other creatures large and small?"

Washington, D.C., zoo director Michael Robinson may best express the role of zoos today. He says, "We've gone from being consumers of wildlife to being producers of wildlife."

Does this testimonial support the author's point? Why or why not?

What propaganda technique is being used here?

Should zoos protect endangered species?

The author uses several testimonials in this viewpoint. How effective are they in supporting her main idea? After reading this viewpoint, do you think zoos are necessary? Why or why not?

Editor's Note: In the following viewpoint, the author argues that zoos are not capable of helping endangered species. The author quotes experts in different fields to prove his case. As you read try to determine whether these quotations make the argument more convincing.

What slanted words do you find in this paragraph?

Does this testimonial support the author's main idea, that zoos do not protect endangered species?

There is no truth to the claim that zoos are the saviors of the world's endangered species. In fact, zoos endanger some species, and they are ill-equipped to be the saviors of others. Zoos are not modern-day Noah's Arks, nor should they be.

Extinction has been a part of the natural world since time began. A brief study of the fossil record shows that over time millions of species have been lost. Norman D. Levine is a professor of veterinary medicine in Urbana, Illinois. He says, "Perhaps 95 percent of the species that once existed no longer exist."

© Carol Simpson/Rothco.

Conservationists tell us that today dozens of species die each day. It is true that many of these extinctions are caused by human actions. People destroy natural habitat, hunt, cut down trees, use environmental poisons such as pesticides, and so forth. Yet extinction is such a natural event that one must question whether it would be wise to try to stop it. Professor Levine says, "Extinction comes from failure to adapt to a changing environment. . . . What the species preservers are trying to do is stop the clock. It cannot and should not be done. Extinction. . . is needed for progress. New species continually arise, and they are better adapted to their environment than those that have died out."

Another argument against preserving endangered species is that we may want some of them to become extinct. Of the thousands that die out each year, many are disease carriers that endanger humans, plants, and other animals; some are disease organisms themselves. Dr. Levine points out, "The smallpox virus has been eliminated. . . . Should it be brought back?" He also comments on the less dangerous species that have become extinct: "Would it improve Earth if even half of the species that have died out were to return? A few starving, shipwrecked sailors might be better off if the dodo were to return, but I would not be." Even if zoos were capable of saving species such as these, would we want them to?

Merritt Clifton is an environmental journalist. He writes, "Zoos must conserve species indefinitely, in finite space with finite budgets." He means that zoos have the resources to care for only a limited number of animals. Colin Rawlins of London's Zoological Society points out that "the cost of keeping all the rare animals in zoos is at least $15 million a year."

Even the largest zoos cannot house more than a couple of hundred animals among the millions that exist. Of the species they house, they may have only one animal of a certain species, a pair or two of another. Zoological experts tell us that in order to save an endangered species, a zoo would have to successfully breed the animals and then reintroduce them to their natural habitat. There are several problems with this.

1. Often there is no suitable habitat to reintroduce them to. The Amazon rainforest, for example, home of thousands of species, grows smaller daily by several hundred acres. At the present rate, in a few more decades the rainforest will no longer exist. What will then be done with the rainforest species "saved" by zoo breeding?

© Zoological Society of San Diego

What propaganda technique is Dr. Levine using?

Do these testimonials support the author's viewpoint? How can you tell?

What propaganda technique is used in this paragraph?

2. Reintroducing a species to its natural environment is difficult, if not impossible. Zoo animals are used to being fed by others and to living in enclosed areas. They do not know how to survive in the wilderness. Ken Chisholm is an animal dealer in Montreal. He laughs at the idea of returning zoo-raised animals to the wild. "Sure. Send [back to the Arctic] the polar bears. . .that have been kept in captivity for twenty years in a warm climate," he says. "They don't know how to swim, they don't know how to hunt, they don't have any fat—they're going to freeze or starve to death before you fly home."

3. In order to preserve a species, it is not enough to breed a pair of the animals each year, hoping that each breeding session will succeed. A zoo would have to breed dozens or hundreds of pairs to stop a species from becoming extinct. Zoo breeding programs have been notoriously unsuccessful. Until recent years, it has been the exception rather than the rule for captive animals to breed successfully. Out of their natural surroundings, animals lose their natural instincts and behavior patterns. They become depressed and lethargic. They become susceptible to unusual diseases. And they generally fail to breed.

By showing only the negative side of zoo breeding, what propaganda technique is the author using?

A good example is the delightful Chinese pandas housed at the Washington D.C. zoo. One panda belonged to the zoo; the second was borrowed from China for breeding purposes. Alas, the pair showed no interest in breeding and in fact were antagonistic to each other.

In other cases, zoo animals might breed, only to have unhealthy offspring. Or sometimes the parents do something they probably would not do in the wild: They kill the babies.

BLOOM COUNTY   by Berke Breathed

4. Another kind of problem deals with inbreeding and supply-and-demand. With the limited numbers of animals in a given zoo, breeding programs are in danger of doing too much inbreeding—using one male to impregnate a couple of females *and* their offspring and *their* offspring, and so forth. The lack of new bloodlines leads to weaker species and often to problems with health, mental fitness, and fertility.

   Today, to reduce this problem, zoos trade animals among themselves for breeding purposes. A breeding animal from one zoo is sent to another to add new blood to each zoo's lines. But there are limitations here too. One is that animals do not like being transported to new environments. Another is that many times animals from different zoos don't like each other and will not breed. A third is that there simply are not enough animals of a certain species to prevent them from being endangered.

5. Finally, no zoo has room for dozens or hundreds of animals of the same species. Zoos need a variety of animals. This is why people pay to go to the zoo. Thus, a zoo may have room for three hundred Pere David's deer. But instead it must use the space for a pair or two of these all-but-extinct deer and pairs or small groups of several dozen other species.

All of these factors lead to only one possible conclusion: Zoos are not the way to preserve endangered species. By their nature, they are not equipped to do it. If we wish to make the preservation of endangered species a priority, we will have to find another way.

Can zoos protect endangered species?

The author lists several reasons why it is impractical for zoos to try to be the "saviors" of endangered species. List four of these reasons. Do you find them convincing? After reading viewpoints 5 and 6, which one do you think used more propaganda techniques? Which did you think was more convincing? Did the propaganda techniques influence you to agree with the authors? Explain.

CRITICAL THINKING SKILL 3 Evaluating Testimonials

Many speakers and writers quote or paraphrase the ideas of famous people and experts. They usually use these testimonials to add weight to their own argument. But many times the testimonials are irrelevant. This is why it is important to examine testimonials to see if they really do support the argument.

Below are several examples of an author using quotations and paraphrases in an article about zoos and endangered species. Mark each one according to the following code:

© Zoological Society of San Diego

G for good use of a testimonial

P for poor testimonial; using a celebrity without consideration of his/her knowledge of the topic

I for irrelevant testimonial; has nothing to do with the topic under discussion

N for not a testimonial; a quotation that simply provides information and is not intended to add weight to a particular view

EXAMPLE: The head of the American Zoological Association says that over 125 million people visit zoos each year. This support from the public proves zoos can save endangered species.

ANSWER: *I*—attendance at zoos has nothing to do with endangered species.

Answers

1. Kiefer Bowen, an actor who once played a zookeeper on a television show, says that zoos play an important role in preserving endangered species. ____

2. The head of the American Zoological Association says that zoos must put their resources to work to save endangered species. ____

3. Sylvia Elston is the author of *The Endangered Species Source Book*. She says that more than a thousand species become extinct every year. ____

4. Primates International is an organization dedicated to the preservation of monkeys, chimpanzees, and other primates. The organization's director says that zoos have made it possible to ____

Answers

preserve several rare kinds of primates and to reintroduce them to their natural habitats.

5. Professor Norman Levine, an expert on extinction, says that zoos have no business trying to save endangered species. He believes that extinction is a natural part of the process of evolution. ____

6. An author quotes her neighbor, who recently traveled to Africa. The neighbor says that she sees more gorillas in zoos than she saw in Africa. ____

7. The head of the American Dental Association says that without zoos our children may never see a rare mountain gorilla. ____